Dear Parents/Caregivers:

Children learn to read in stages, and all children develop reading skills at different ages. **Fisher-Price® Ready Reader Storybooks**™ were created to encourage children's interest in reading and to increase their reading skills. The stories in this series were written to specific grade levels to serve the needs of children from preschool through third grade. Of course, every child is different, so we hope that you will allow your child to explore the stories at his or her own pace.

Book 1 and Book 2: Most Appropriate For Preschoolers

Book 3 and Book 4: Most Appropriate For Kindergartners

Book 5 and Book 6: Most Appropriate For First Graders

Book 7 and Book 8: Most Appropriate For Second Graders

Book 9 and Book 10: Most Appropriate For Third Graders

All of the stories in this series are fun, easy-to-follow tales that have engaging full-color artwork. Children can move from Books 1 and 2, which have the simplest vocabulary and concepts, to each progressive level to expand their reading skills. With the **Fisher-Price® Ready Reader Storybooks**™, reading will become an exciting adventure for your child. Soon your child will not only be ready to read, but will be eager to do so.

Educational Consultants: Mary McLean-Hely, M.A. in Education: Design and Evaluation of Educational Programs, Stanford University; Wendy Gelsanliter, M.S. in Early Childhood Education, Bank Street College of Education; Nancy A. Dearborn, B.S. in Education, University of Wisconsin-Whitewater

Fisher-Price® Ready Reader Storybook™

Tappy's Team

Book 6

Written by Nicole O'Neill • Illustrated by Art Mawhinney

Modern Publishing
A Division of Unisystems, Inc.
New York, New York 10022

I'm going to try out for a team.

To be an athlete is my dream.

I'll practice hard. I'll sweat and train.

I can play any game!

9

The baseball team seems like fun.

So, over to the field I run.

We have practice every day.
I can't wait to really play.

Today is our very first game.
On my new uniform is my name!

13

The ball is coming!
It's almost here!

I didn't catch it but I hear a cheer.

15

"No sweat, Tappy," says Coach Ted,
"Telly caught the ball instead."

Now I step up to the plate.

My swing missed. It was too late.

"That's OK," says Coach Ted, "Tubby scored. We're still ahead."

21

But I want to score a run.

Otherwise, it's just no fun!

23

Coach says that's not what a team is about.

We have to help each other out.

We will cheer when you score.

That's what a baseball team is for.

My next time up I hit the ball.
It goes all the way to the wall!

Playing baseball is just great and the best part is my teammates!

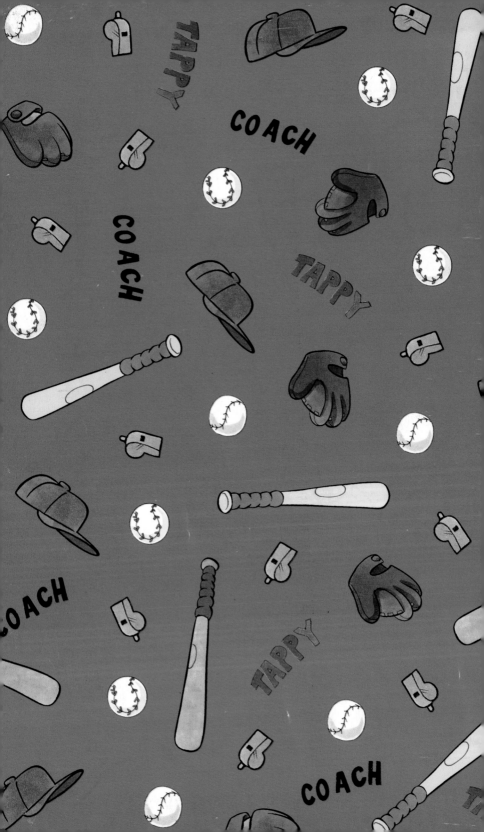